TIGERS

WILDLIFE IN DANGER

Louise Martin

Rourke Publishing LLC
Vero Beach, Florida 32964

www.rourkepublishing.com

PHOTO CREDITS:
Cover Photo © Lynn M. Stone

EDITORIAL SERVICES:
Pamela Schroeder

Library of Congress Cataloging-in-Publication Data

Martin, Louise, 1955–
    Tigers / Louise Martin.
        p. cm. — (Wildlife in danger)
    Includes index
    ISBN 1-58952-023-8
    1. Tigers—Juvenile literature. 2. Endangered species—Juvenile literature.
    [I. Tigers. 2. Endangered species.] I.Title

QL737.C23 M276 2001
599.756—dc21

                                                    00-067070

Printed in the USA

TABLE OF CONTENTS

TIGERS

Tigers are the largest of wild cats. They are also one of the largest **carnivores**, or meat-eating animals, in the world. The biggest of tigers may weigh up to 660 pounds (300 kilograms).

Tigers are not just big. They arc beautiful. But thousands of tigers have been killed for their beautiful fur. The tigers' beauty is one reason that they are **endangered**. Endangered animals are in danger of becoming **extinct**. Animals that become extinct, like the dinosaurs, disappear forever.

Tigers look like big, striped house cats

WHERE TIGERS LIVE

Wild tigers live in certain parts of many Asian countries. The kinds of places where tigers can find food, shelter, and safety are called **habitats**. Tigers live in many different habitats, from swamps and grasslands to mountain forests. Tigers hunt several different kinds of animals, as **prey**, including deer, wild hogs, and wild cattle.

A tiger laps water from a pond

Tiger habitats have shrunk a lot in just the past 100 years. The only country with more than 1,000 wild tigers is India. Smaller numbers of wild tigers live in Nepal, Bhutan, Myanmar, Bangladesh, Thailand, Lao PDR, Cambodia, Vietnam, Malaysia, Indonesia, China, and perhaps North Korea.

The exact number of wild tigers remaining is unknown. In 1998, scientists believed there were between 5,000 and 7,500. In 1900, there may have been 100,000 wild tigers!

A tiger's keen eyesight helps it find prey

TIGERS IN DANGER

Hunting sharply reduced the number of tigers during the 20th century. Hunting wild tigers is now against the law, but tigers still face big problems.

One problem is the growing number of people in Asia. People make new farms, towns, and neighborhoods. Tiger habitat and prey disappear. In India, for example, there are about six people today for every one person in 1900.

*Tigers in warm areas cool off
by taking a swim*

The Indian tiger population is growing

A pair of Chinese tigers in Shanghai Zoo

Tigers, of course, can be dangerous to people. No one wants a wild tiger in the backyard. As a result, wild tigers now live mostly on lands called **reserves**. Reserves are places set aside to protect wild animals.

But even tigers in reserves are not always safe. **Poachers** sneak into reserves to kill tigers for their fur and body parts. Poachers are people who kill animals even when it is against the law.

A Bengal tiger relaxes with her cub

Tiger bones and other body parts are sold as medicine in many parts of Asia. Tiger parts don't really cure people of anything. But for hundreds of years, some Asians have believed that certain animal parts are strong medicine. They are willing to pay high prices for wild animal parts. The money makes the poachers willing to risk fines or jail.

A tiger's stripes help it blend into the plants around it

TIGER TYPES

Tigers from throughout Asia are much alike. They all belong to the same cat group. But tigers in some places are larger, darker, or more furry than tigers in other places. The tigers from cold, far eastern Russia, for example, can weigh twice as much as the tigers from the warm island of Sumatra.

Scientists call these slightly different types of tigers **subspecies**. Five subspecies of tigers remain. Three subspecies became extinct during the 20th century.

Like house cats, tigers spend much of their time napping or resting

The most endangered of the subspecies is the South China tiger. Perhaps fewer than 20 remain in the wild. Only 48 survive in zoos.

Scientists in 1998 guessed that just 330 to 370 Siberian, or Amur, tigers remained in the wild. The number of Sumatran tigers was probably 400 to 500 with about 1,227 to 1,785 Indo-Chinese tigers. Bengal, or Indian, tiger numbers were between 3,200 and 4,700.

A tiger stands over its prey in an Indian reserve

SAVING TIGERS

Asians have long thought of wild animals as food or sport. Saving wild animals is a fairly new idea. And most Asian countries are poor. Still, some countries are now making great efforts to save their few wild tigers.

These countries are getting help from others. The Save The Tiger Fund, for example, started in 1995. It has put money into 112 projects. The Save The Tiger Fund has received dollars from the Exxon Mobil Corporation, the National Fish and Wildlife Foundation, and thousands of school children and adults.

GLOSSARY

carnivore (KAR nuh vor) — a meat-eating animal, such as a tiger

endangered (en DANE jerd) — to be in danger of becoming extinct

extinct (ex TINKT) — having disappeared altogether; no longer existing

habitat (HAB uh tat) — the certain type of place where an animal naturally lives, such as a rain forest

poacher (PO chur) — one who kills animals that are protected by law

prey (PRAY) — an animal that is hunted by another animal for food

reserve (re ZERV) — a place set aside to protect wild animals

subspecies (SUB spee sheez) — a slightly different group within a larger, closely related group, such as a Siberian tiger

INDEX